HISTORICAL
FALCONRY
AN ILLUSTRATED GUIDE

ANDREW
AND HELEN STEWART

AMBERLEY

In honour and memory of our dear, departed friend Robb Hoseason
(21 April 1966 to 7 August 2013)

First published 2015

Amberley Publishing
The Hill, Stroud,
Gloucestershire, GL5 4EP

www.amberley-books.com

ISBN 978 1 4456 5114 9 (print)
ISBN 978 1 4456 5115 6 (ebook)

British Library Cataloguing in Publication Data.
A catalogue record for this book is available from the British Library.

Typeset in 11pt on 14pt Celeste.
Typesetting by Amberley Publishing.
Printed in the UK.

Contents

Acknowledgements

Naturally, having embarked on this journey into the past for ten years now, we imagine the first people we have to thank are the team of amazing birds with whom we have lived our life. Without them and without their steadfast dedication and natural brilliance, what we do, what we strive to achieve, would simply not be possible.

A vast amount of thanks must also go to our fantastic group of followers on our online group – 'Friends of Albion Historical Falconry'. You are a bunch of inspirational people with such a desire to learn, it is so fulfilling and rewarding to help be a part of that. Some of you have offered support above and beyond what could ever have been expected of you, and our gratitude runs deeper than you will ever understand.

A big shout of gratitude, in particular, must go of course to our photographers. You all spent a lot of time and effort reformatting pictures to the right size and resolutions – a thankless task, we know! Our fantastic photographers who provided images for the book are:

Nigel Morgan (who not only provided images for the inside, but also the front and rear covers!)
Peter Gillatt
Tom Wardrop
Andrew Macfetters
Pat Patrick
Ian Hennah
Wayne and Louise Arnett
Paul Trask
Jim Thompson
Jemma Marsh
Gareth Howell
and Gail Hilton

Also, a thank you to Zoe Spencer Fine Art Prints, for her Peregrine Falcon head-study.

A final thank you must go to all of our clients, who have supported our venture over the years and provided us with an outlet to share our work and research. In particular, we must thank The National Trust, who have helped us to raise our success.

Historical portraits and images supplied by the British Library open content, Yale Centre for British Art, the NEA, and Getty Open Images.

Peregrine falcon by Zoe Spencer.

Foreword

Modern falconry is a far cry from what our ancestors knew and practiced in times past. The way in which falconry is practiced today fits very well into the busy, hurried and cosmopolitan lifestyle experienced by modern man. Given that a newly caught up falcon comes to one in a rather wild and untame fashion, it is far easier to control the bird, and to train it, by following modern methodologies of reducing the food intake until the bird's hunger (which is a strong impulse in a predatory species that needs to be satisfied) becomes a stronger urge to satiate than the urge to escape from the falconer. A bird will respond to the falconer's wishes far sooner when feeling hungry, and therefore the time needed to acclimatise, condition and tame the bird is significantly reduced. So it is clear to see why, in the twenty-first century, modern falconers comfortably train birds in this fashion.

A royalist lady with a kestrel.

Historically, however, the lifestyle and culture of ancient man could not be more different, and falconry was considered to be a way of life, not just a hobby or interest to be pursued when time constraints allowed. The trade in hawks and falcons across the world was a vast and major industry, and your choice of bird, and its prowess in the field, were clearly representative of your social standing. In fact, birds of prey were put on a pedestal historically. Quite unlike a horse or a hound, they were seen as a creature that had to be shown respect and worked with like a partner – this is evident in the phraseology 'to break a horse' and 'to make a hawk'.

Therefore, historically, instead of being trained using the modern 'food monitoring' and 'weight reduction' methods, a newly caught wild bird would be offered as much good-quality food as possible, in order to demonstrate to the bird over a significant period of time that it need not fear the falconer, that it was shown a vast degree of respect, and that, moreover, it was getting a 'better deal' with the falconer than it had experienced in the wild. While this was a more labour-intensive system of management, which often saw the training of a falcon or hawk take several months (in contrast to modern falconry, where a falconer may claim to train a bird in ten days), it was the modus operandi for our historical counterparts.

An Elizabethan gentleman.

A Tudor lady, relaxing in contemplation of a noble falcon.

To explain this in the depth that we feel would do justice to the complexity of these methods would require an entire book in itself (... after all, we have been researching this for over a decade and have worked from around fifty separate treatises, so to encompass all of this in the space of this book would simply not be possible!), but some of the main treatises from which we work will be discussed in later pages.

Needless to say, there are still many historical treatises and sources to be discovered out there, all of which will undoubtedly hold a wealth of information that, as a whole, has not been practiced in the United Kingdom since before the Victorian era. If we are not careful, traditional falconry – its mantras, methodologies and techniques that we have researched – are in danger of being lost to the ravages of time. Of course, these techniques of which we speak can be read from manuscripts, but we believe that a lot can be lost in translation between page and practice, and it has taken a unique blend of our love and understanding of historical culture and lifestyle as a whole – and our knowledge of falconry, this most delicate art form – to bring these lost skills back to life.

We have both found that there seemed to be a niche within the heritage research and education sector for credible, accurate falconry displays, using exclusively historically accurate species of birds that have been naturally reared by their parents (not imprinted on man) and trained using the traditional skills. We have attempted to fill this niche with our research, but also our passions for history, for

A saker falcon in flight.

A Viking falconer in silhouette.

falconry and for the preservation of the heritage of both. We decided a decade ago to start collecting copies of the historical treatises and manuscripts that still exist relating to the subject of falconry. Our quest for knowledge has, over time, also extended to collecting copies of artwork, poetry and prose all relating to falconry, delving into household accounts of famous falconers from the past, and studying the intertwined links between historical falconry and the other aspects of ancient culture.

A lanner falcon returning to the fist of his falconer.

By doing so, we hope that our work will go some small measure of the way to keeping this dying tradition – this lost art – alive, or perhaps inspire the next generation of falconers, historians and conservationists to strive beyond the parameters set down for us by modern society, and to look beyond, to the knowledge we have lost to the past.

The authors as Tudor falconers: Andrew as an Elizabethan falconer and Helen as a Henrician lady.

Origins ... The First Whispers of Falconry

Falconry is our most noble and ancient field sport. The first question most people ask about historical falconry is: when was it first practiced?

The first, and by far the earliest, possible evidence we have for falconry being practiced comes from a small piece of cave art, found in Golpaygan in central Iran. This shows an image of a falconer, with a bird upon his fist, riding on a horse with a hunting dog, and this dates back to 10000–8000 BC. Recent excavations in Sumeria have also discovered skeletons of hunting hounds alongside those of birds of prey, dating from 8000–7000 BC, and these burials were associated with civilised areas.

Sketch of cave art from Goypaygan in Iran, showing a mounted falconer, dating from 10000–8000 BC.

The earliest certified evidence we have for falconry being practiced worldwide comes from the third millennium BC. This takes the form of a sliver of pottery showing a raptor on the fist of a man wearing jesses. This was uncovered from Tell Chuera in Syria.

By 2400–2100 BC we have possible evidence of falconry in England from a Beaker burial that was discovered as part of the Lord Londesborough excavation in 1851 at Kelleythorpe, Driffield, in east Yorkshire. In burial cist thirty-eight of a multi-burial barrow, a skeleton was found with various burial artefacts. These included a pottery beaker (characterising it as a 'Beaker' burial), a copper dagger and a side-looped bone toggle (65.5 mm long and 14 mm wide at the loop). Of greater interest, with regards to falconry, were a stone wristguard, worn on the arm of the skeleton and studded with copper rivets, and a skull of a hawk, placed close to the wristguard.

Woodward and Hunter (in their 2011 work *An Examination of Stone Bracers from Britain*) theorise that this burial and the items contained within it are related to an early Bronze Age falconer. In the Middle East, falconers have always used, and still use today, the 'mangalah' – a reinforced sleeve or cuff designed to protect the wearer from the talons or claws of the falcon or hawk. With this in mind, the studded stone wristguard may be indicative of an early form of mangalah-like cuff, used to protect this ancient man from the damaging effects of his bird's feet, especially when found in relation to, and close proximity with, the skull of a hawk (and a bone toggle of unknown use) within this burial.

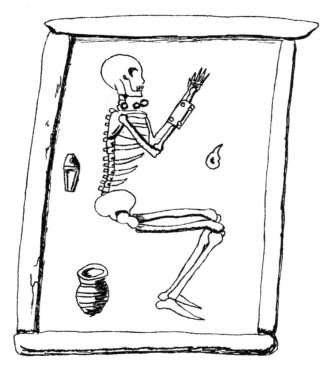

Sketch of the Beaker burial, with the stone wristguard and the hawk skull shown.

A male saker falcon about to stoop.

Saker falcon stooping.

However, one of the problems encountered when trying to identify falconry in the earlier periods of history is the lack of archaeological finds that can directly indicate the captive management of birds of prey. Bird bones, being by nature very hollow and fragile, do not preserve well when buried, often dissolving in acidic soils to the point where no trace of them is left behind.

While excavating Danebury Hillfort in Hampshire, Dr Barry Culiffe and his team uncovered pits dating back to the Iron Age that appear to be some form of depository for animal remains, for they contained bones from a variety of animals, including sheep, cattle, dogs and, most interestingly, birds. The majority of bird bones came from crows, but also to be found within the collection were skeletal remains from a common buzzard (*Buteo Buteo*) and red kites (*Milvus Milvus*), both of which are scavengers that are often found in urbanised and rural dig sites throughout Britain. Perhaps more noteworthy were the remains of a European kestrel (*Falcon Tinnunculus*) and a peregrine falcon (*Falcon Peregrinus*). Although, unfortunately, neither sets of these remains contained the leg bones that would have possibly helped identify them as birds used for falconry, as a study could have been carried out to see if there were any worn patches on the bone from being tethered, for example.

It seems unlikely to imagine that a peregrine falcon or a kestrel would have been a source of food for Iron Age peoples, so, alternatively, were they buried for a ritualistic reason, as ancient cultures worshipped birds of prey?

A female kestrel (*Falco Tinnunculus*).

Examining them in context with their wider surroundings can often give a better idea for the reason behind their presence in the burial pit. For example, if an Icelandic gyrfalcon was found in an archaeological site in England, historians could be confident that was an example of captive management, since the bird does not occur in England naturally and would have needed to have been imported. The problem in the 'Danebury Hillfort' scenario is that all the raptor skeletons discovered there are native to the British Isles. A closer inspection can be offered by investigating their natural habitats in relation to the area in which they were found and the age of the dig site.

Until very recently, the peregrine falcon was generally found living along the British coastlines, preferring open spaces. Therefore, remains found in an urban settlement are very unusual, particularly in relation to Danebury, which is located far from the coast. The surrounding area would also have been heavily wooded during the Iron Age. This would give a strong indication that the bird in question was undergoing some form of captive management by these individuals living at the hillfort, though whether this was for falconry or some other purpose remains unknown.

There have been many noteworthy archaeological finds from Viking and Saxon sites. One burial contains a female goshawk (as noted by Sadler, 1990) that had slight exotoses on the left tarsometarus, which is believed to be the result of trauma caused by being tethered or handled while wearing jesses. Another goshawk from the same study shows what is described as 'a possible false joint forming on the dorsal end of the left coracoid.' This is an injury occasionally seen in modern

A female peregrine falcon (*Falco Peregrinus*).

A pair of falconers from the Viking era.

falconry birds and is indicative of a bird having been tethered with too long a leash, allowing a long 'bate' for the bird to jump. The break in this hawk's bone was well healed, which shows good evidence for the bird having been a captive falconry bird as a wild bird would likely die were it to suffer a similar injury due to its inability to hunt effectively.

Another way in which historians can be confident that the finds demonstrate captive falconry usage of the birds is the ratio between the genders of the bird skeletons and bones discovered. The remains that are found are predominantly female, and, considering the fact that the female is the gender often chosen for use in falconry, owing to its size and ferocity, it would seem to indicate that these birds were managed in captivity for use as hunting birds. In a 2001 study, Annia Cherryson made comparisons between the raptor species found in dig sites and the quarry species found alongside them. There was clear correlation between the two, which can be seen particularly well, for example, from the remains at Castle Rising, from the twelfth to the fifteenth centuries, which contained the remains of a sparrowhawk, goshawk and peregrine falcon, and then also contained quarry species including hare, rabbit, mallard, teal, wigeon, heron, crane, plover, curlew, woodcock, moorhen, partridge, pheasant, woodpigeon, rock doves, song thrush, blackbirds and redwings.

When all of the above factors are related to one another within their proper context, researchers can gain a relatively confident synopsis on the use of a bird for falconry.

A mature female peregrine falcon displaying the typical blue colouring of the species in adulthood.

By 2205 BC there are records from the Heian dynasty in China of birds being given as gifts in the royal court. By 1700 BC, wall hangings and pictorial records provide evidence of Persian and Arabic falconry, while Assyrian Bas-relief art shows hawks being trapped from 722 BC. By 680 BC, Chinese records were detailing falconry and its practice in detail.

In Europe, the first definitive records of falconry describe the Goths learning the skills and practice of the art from the Sarmatians. Aristotle, the famous Greek philosopher, mentions falconry between 384 and 322 BC. The first records of falconry in Japan are from AD 355 with the Nihon Shoki narrative, which describes hawks arriving in Japan during the reign of Emperor Nintoku.

The fifth century saw Avitus, from the Celtic tribe of the Arverni, become Roman emperor between AD 455 and AD 456. He fought at the Battle of Châlons with the Goths, against the Huns, and it was he who appears to have introduced falconry to the Roman Empire. With the Roman Empire, we see the first definitive traces of falconry in Britain.

It is clear to see that the art of hunting with birds of prey has always been held in great prestige, even as early as the third millennium BC, and this wondrous art appears to have originated in, and spread from, the Middle and Far East. It makes perfect sense that as humans migrated across Europe from the east, to farm and find new lands, that they brought the skills with them to the west.

Historians know that Europeans were travelling to Turkey as early as the third century BC, and there were as many as 10,000 Celts living in Gordion, Anatolia.

A medieval falconer exercising a falcon.

Since falconry had its roots out in these Eastern provinces, one can only make supposition as to whether the Western individuals who certainly lived there, and obviously witnessed this art, also practiced it as well.

The term falconry is a generalisation of the art of hunting with wild birds of prey. It can be split into two distinct types of hunting – 'hawking' (the art of an austringer hunting quarry with a hawk), and 'falconry' (the art of a falconer hunting quarry with a falcon).

Depiction of a fourteenth-century falconer washing the plumage of his bird.

An austringer is the hunter that trains, flies and hunts with hawks (birds of the genus *accipiter*) and, historically, was responsible for bringing in food for the kitchens and table. In Britain there are but two species of Hawk native to these islands: the goshawk (*accipiter gentilis*) and the sparrowhawk (*accipiter nisus*). Both of these species of hawk are closely related to one another, although rather different in size, and are prolific hunters and killers, making them exceptionally practical for hunting for food. In fact, they were so good at bringing quarry to the table that in medieval France the goshawk was known as the 'cook's bird'.

By nature, our two native hawk species are very shy and secretive birds who prefer to retreat to the cover of thick, dense, coniferous woodland, making them very difficult to train and work with around any number of people. In Gace de la Vigne's *Roman des Deduis*, the austringer is described as a lone hunter who is coarse in appearance, hunched and secretive. He is said to be as unapproachable as the bird he handles and indiscriminate in his choice of quarry, spoiling the sport for his betters. However, his redeeming quality was his ability to use his bird to fill the larder with food. Continuing on the theme of the unsightly austringer, Gace writes:

> When one sees an ill-formed man with great big feet and long shapeless shanks, built like a trestle, hump shouldered and skew-backed, and one wants to mock him, one says 'Look! What an austringer!' I know the austringers would like to beat me for this, but there are two dozen of us falconers to each one of them, so I have no fear. Nonetheless, it is a wise man who keeps a Goshawk in his house – a good kitchen bird that it is!

In utter contrast to the austringers were the falconers. The falconer was a professional who specialised in training the hunting falcons for the upper classes of society. He was said to be a very sociable fellow, far more stable in nature than the austringer – rather like the comparison between the skittish hawks and the mellow falcons themselves. He was expected to train the falcons to perform high-quality sporting flights so that his employer, a member of the nobility, might impress and entertain his visiting guests.

The kill ratio of a falcon, in comparison to that of a hawk, is very poor. Also, the high-flying falcons have a tendency to bring down their kill a long way away from the observing falconer, and the hunt itself therefore required an array of hunting dogs (those that could point, those that could flush, and those that could scent) and also trained horses to help the falconer and his party to retrieve the bird. Naturally, these hounds and horses required equal attendees to care for them, making the practice of falconry a far more ostentatious affair than the practice of hawking, where the hawks offered far shorter and less sporting flights, yet with a greater success rate on the kill.

From very early on in history, the flying and hunting of the falcons became more about politics and status, rather than hunting for food. Falcons were imported at

A female Viking falconer flying a falcon.

great cost from around the globe, and were often given as dowries for wedding arrangements or to seal treaties or agreements. The possession of such birds was a clear statement of one's wealth, power and social standing. When visiting ambassadors and dignitaries came from rival kings or emperors, a day spent hunting with one's falcons would be just the trick to impress upon them that perhaps invading the country was not such a good idea; the king being able to afford such prestigious birds surely reflected upon the size of army he could field!

In addition to this, the hunting abilities of the bird in the field would also give a good insight into the psychology of the king or nobleman who flew the bird. In rather similar fashion to the famous phrase 'like dog, like owner', the falcon was a reflection of the human hunting partner that they shared their time with. Therefore, the prowess of the bird on the kill was a good demonstration to any rival that this was someone who shouldn't be messed with. With this in mind, it is clear to see why falconry was such an important pastime in the historical world, and why any member of high society would go to all four corners of the known world to try to import the largest, most aggressive falcons available.

In modern falconry you will often hear it said that a bird of prey is incapable of feelings, and that they will therefore never bond with their falconers. In history, the opinion on this matter was the polar opposite. The techniques used in the past relied upon the fact that the bird was capable of appreciating the efforts of the falconer or austringer to make her comfortable, and it was said that a bird was not ready to be released free from her bonds until she was made 'in love' with her

Above: A saker falcon pouncing upon the lure.

Right: A royalist Civil War gentleman admiring a saker falcon.

These two shots of a saker falcon taking off from the fist display the impressive wing beats he makes in order to take flight. The first shows the saker launching off the fist.

The second shows the first powerful beat of his wings.

A saker falcon in flight.

trainer. This is aptly described by Edmund Bert in his late sixteenth-century work *The Treatise of the Shortwinged Hawk*, in which he writes:

> It may be some young professor in this art is possessed that if his hawk be very hungry and sharp, she will sooner come unto him. He is herein much deceived, for, unless she loves him very well, hunger will be the means that draws her away from him, for her hunger must be satisfied, and her little love of him will make her better pleased to provide for herself, and make her look out for her own provisions.

With some of the proven known origins of falconry in Britain during the Saxon period, the birds were trained using techniques which are, in their essence, not dissimilar from those used in modern times. The understanding of the bird of prey was very basic at the time, and thus birds were trained using food reduction techniques. This encouraged the bird to acquiesce to the falconer's demands so that it might satisfy its hunger.

During the First Crusade, when many members of the nobility were travelling out to the Middle East, falconers were beginning to learn techniques for training birds from the Eastern Islamic peoples that allowed them to feed the bird copious amounts of food while extending the training period, thus creating a better relationship between falconer and bird. This was a rather intensive bonding period between the two, but the benefit was, obviously, a more content bird.

Also, a well-fed, muscular bird is far more able to exhibit impressive natural flight styles and manoeuvres, and to take larger and stronger quarry, than a bird who has had its condition reduced to force obedience. More and more falconry techniques were being learnt throughout this time from the Muslim falconers and, as such, the European and British falconers were bringing home with them not only Eastern birds, like the saker falcon, but also Eastern skills. These skills were then used from the late Norman period right up until the early 1700s, when falconry in Britain was all but forgotten.

By the time falconry was revived as a sport in the Victorian era, it seemed the learning, knowledge and skills of our forefathers had been lost as falconers had reverted back to their Saxon roots in using the weight control and food reduction techniques that are still prevalent in Western falconry today.

The remainder of this book will seek to chart that journey.

Falconry in Late Antiquity Britain – Roman Falconry

Although the Roman period has far less evidence of falconry than other later historical period, there is nevertheless enough evidence to be certain of its existence.

The depiction of Roman falconry in British sculpture suggests an influence from the Middle East. The earliest example of pictorial evidence of Roman falconry in Europe is the floor mosaic in Argos, Greece, in the aptly named 'Villa of the Falconer', dating to AD 500. As few pictorial examples still exist from the Roman period, and though we can prove they did indeed practice falconry, it seems to not have been a widely practiced art.

It is widely believed that falconry was introduced to the Romans by the Visigoths, who invaded the Mediterranean area around AD 400 and, at the very least, the Romanised ruling classes who had settled throughout Gaul had certainly adopted the sport.

It is evident that falconry was well established by the sixth century BC as the Franks had listed regulations for the sport in the *Lex Salica*. The Romans also adopted the Imperial Eagle, with all its power and might, as the symbol of their entire empire, thus showing respect and awe of the prowess of this mighty hunting bird.

In 1994, a small amount of bird bones were discovered in a Roman midden from the third and fourth century within the grounds of a villa situated at Great Holts Farm, Boreham, Essex. Cattle bones were the most common finds, but more importantly were the discoveries of the bones of a sparrowhawk along with the bones of its prey, a thrush, within the pit. This could possibly be very early evidence of Roman falconry in Britain (as described by Parker, 1998), and sparrowhawk bones are only rarely found on Roman sites. They are more commonly found in sites dating to a later period than the one described above. The reasons given for associating the skeleton with falconry is the fact that sparrowhawks are not scavengers who would be likely to die randomly within the confines of a villa, and they are too small to have been considered worthwhile for meat for consumption or for their feathers.

Roman Imperial Eagle worked from bronze, found in Asia and dating AD 100–300.

The Romans, generally, were not keen on the idea of falconry – all evidence for falconry in the Roman Empire comes from the outer reaches of the empire where the majority of the populace living under Roman rule were subjugated natives who had perhaps already practiced falconry prior to being invaded or conquered, and there is little to no evidence to suggest that falconry was practiced in Italy or Rome itself.

Roman oil lamp in terracotta depicting an Imperial Eagle, AD 200–300, Tunisia.

The earliest official evidence that conclusively proves falconry was practiced during the Roman period comes from Paulinus of Pella, in the fifth century AD. Paulinus was a Christian poet. In his works *Eucharisticon*, he talks about falconry, and this is said to be the oldest know Western literary reference to the art.

Paulinus mentions that his wish as a youth was to possess a horse with fine trappings, a swift dog and a splendid hawk.

In AD 472, Sidonius Appolinarius talks about hawking in the contents of two letters. In the first, while writing to his friend Vetius, he comments about training horses, judging dogs and carrying hawks. In a second letter, written two years later, he again makes reference to his passion for hawks.

One of the most famous of the Roman mosaics relating to falconry is the floor piece dated to AD 500 at Argos in the Peloponese in Greece. The 'Villa of the Falconer' is decorated with scenes of hunting and falconry, which is shown in a pictorial sequence. Beginning with the hunter preparing, then secondly the hunter with a bird alighted upon his fist, then several ducks taking flight, and finally ending with a hawk seizing a duck.

In another scene, taken from the Great Palace of Constantinople, a hawk is shown on its quarry. This dates to the late fifth or early sixth century. Finally, there is a manuscript dating to the late Roman period that mimics the Constantinople mosaic, showing a falconer waiting under a tree watching his hawk clutch a small bird wit has caught.

The lanner falcon. Lanners can be found naturally in Italy, and Roman people would have been familiar with them, but it is doubtful whether they flew them or not.

This peregrine tiercel (male) is named Vercingetorix, after the famous Gallic cheiftain who stood up to the Romans. He was eventually defeated by Julius Caesar at the Battle of Alesia.

Roman falconry was, therefore, clearly practiced, but with far less zeal and enthusiasm than in later periods of history, and it was almost certainly confined to far-flung parts of the empire in which natives, who had likely practiced the art prior to Roman rule, continued on with the sport after being amalgamated into the Roman world. It can be said that, unless further evidence is uncovered in the future, nothing is known about the types of techniques and methods used to train the birds in the Roman era.

Peregrine tiercel on the lure.

Viking and Saxon
Dark Age Falconry

Their haufdu Hauko sing a oxlorn
They had hawks on their shoulders
(*Rolf Krakes Saga*)

Some of the best and most sought-after birds can be found in Norway, Scandinavia, Greenland and Iceland. These include the mighty gyrfalcon, the largest species of falcon in the entire world, and the Scandinavian goshawk, who, owing to the chilly and mountainous landscape, have evolved to be larger in size than their southern counterparts, thus making them highly prized across Europe – so much so that they became one of the mainstays of Viking economy.

A Viking man lures a peregrine falcon.

It is a known fact that during the Viking Age, falconry was already established as an aristocratic hunting technique. We can be certain of this from a variety of archaeological finds.

The use of bells upon the birds was probably a result of Eastern Baltic influence, in particular with the Rus Vikings, a Viking people who settled in what is now modern-day Russia. Copper and iron bells appear to have been popular and they are often found alongside birds of prey in the graves of Viking nobility.

In Viking culture, it was said that hunting came second only to fighting as the best and most prestigious form of physical activity. According to Frankish sources, Godfred, the early ninth-century king of the Danes, was killed by his own son while out hunting, just as he was about to release his falcon from its prey.

Furthermore, in the Norse sagas we learn that Earl Hakon had to pay 100 marks of gold and sixty hawks or falcons as tribute to Harald Bluetooth, which shows how falconry was often used in the Viking period to seal political relationships.

There are at least twenty known burials in Scandinavia containing birds of prey, dating from the sixth to the tenth centuries, demonstrating that there was not only a long-running tradition of the practice of falconry in Viking culture, but also a deep respect and bond between the falconer and their bird – so much so that they wanted to remain united, even in death.

A fine example of a Scandinavian goshawk.

A Rus-Viking with a small falcon.

In another cremation grave from AD 800, the remains were discovered of a man, his hunting dog and also his falcon. In an earlier grave from Pillingen, a man had been buried in an extremely richly furnished grave, with his falcon on his right hand. This shows further evidence of a link to Middle Eastern techniques, as Western falconers use the left hand to carry the bird. One can only wonder whether the Vikings were also already using the Eastern falconry techniques as well, as opposed to the rather basic techniques employed by the Saxons.

Pictorial evidence from Norway, Sweden and Uppland display further evidence of falconry in Viking times, including mounted men with hunting hawks upon their fists. Tapestries from the Oseburg ship burial of AD 834 include a scene with a mounted man and two hunting hawks.

The Old Norse *Edda* script gives a good insight into the Viking relationship with birds of prey, and especially the Eagle, with its religious connotations. The poem titled 'Vafpruonismal' explains to us how the god, Odin, gives a challenge to the wisest of the giants – not in physical combat, but rather a combat of knowledge. Even though it is not a physical challenge, it is still a challenge to the death. Odin begins by saying 'For the ninth, tell me, for you seem knowledgeable, Vafpruonir, if you know – Where from comes the wind that whines across the seas? He himself can no man discern.'

Vafpruonir answers 'Hraesvelgr is his name, at the end of the world, sits a giant in the eternal eagles abode, and from his wings the wind is said to come travelling far above folk.'

It was said 'so the eagle, whose name translates as corpse swallower, from his wings arise the wind and the storm.'

Vedrfolnir was said to be the eagle that sits atop Yggdrasil, the Ash tree that was also the 'world tree' in Viking mythology, and between his eyes sat the hawk, Habrok.

Ragnar Lothbrok, the famous ninth-century Viking warrior, was a very adventurous fellow about whom many myths abound and who travelled often from Scandinavia to England. Viking legends say that while hawking along the Danish coast in a small boat, Ragnar was blown by a terrible storm to the shores of England.

He landed in Norfolk, and, because of his great skill and hawking and hunting, he soon became a great favourite of King Edmund of East Anglia and was allowed to reside at his court.

The king's huntsman, Berne, grew very jealous of Ragnar, who he believed had usurped his position in the hunt and at the court and in the king's affections. Berne then, in a fit of rage, killed Ragnar and hid his body.

A sketch showing a mounted Viking falconer from a Swedish stone.

However, Ragnar's faithful greyhound kept watch over his dead master's body and eventually, due to the howling of the dog, the crime was discovered.

Berne was put out to sea in the same boat which Ragnar had arrived upon, and was blown to Denmark by the same unfortunate winds, where the boat was discovered.

Berne was taken before Ragnar's sons, where he accused King Edmund of the murder, and thus Ragnar's sons swore revenge upon the king. They invaded England and they martyred King Edmund. Berne the huntsman got away with his crime!

Like many Viking tales, this is almost certainly a mixture of legend, fable and perhaps a little truth, but it nevertheless demonstrates the importance of falconry in the cultural heritage of the Vikings.

Of course, Viking culture in Britain was closely intertwined with that of the Anglo Saxons, the people living in Britain at the time of the Viking invasions.

The first documented Saxon falconer was the King of Kent, Ethelbert II, in the eighth century, followed by Alfred the Great and then Athelstan in the ninth century. For the Saxons, falconry was not just a method of catching food for the pot – it had also become a prestigious royal sport.

One of the earliest references for birds of prey in Saxon Britain is from Theodore, who, somewhere between AD 668 and 690, wrote 'Birds and other animals that are strangled in nets are not to be eaten by men, nor if they are found

Viking woman putting equipment
back onto a falcon after a flight.

A female peregrine falcon such as this would have been considered to be a fine bird for catching heron and crane.

dead after having been struck down by a hawk.' However, we cannot be sure if the hawks he was referring to were wild or captively managed examples. In any case, the earliest defined reference to falconry comes from the correspondence of St Boniface, the Anglo-Saxon missionary to the continent, who in a letter to King Ethelbald of Mercia in AD 745 wrote, 'Meanwhile, as a sign of our true love and devoted friendship, we have sent you a hawk and two falcons.' Ethelbald replied, 'I wish you to procure for me two falcons whose particular skill and daring in their art shall be to capture cranes.'

There is also the figure of a falconer, dating from AD 685 and carved upon a monumental stone cross, to be found at Bewcastle in Cumberland. Remains of a sparrowhawk were also found in a site at Eltham, Norfolk, from AD 650–850. By the late eighth century, hawkers were members of the royal household. Kings of England enjoyed falconry throughout the eighth to tenth centuries. King Alfred the Great was known to be an avid falconer and had austringers and falconers as part of his household – he even wrote a book on falconry. Athelstan was also another avid falconer, who included hawks and falcons in his diplomatic arrangements. He forced the rulers of north Wales to pay him an annual tribute of 'birds trained to make prey of other birds in the air.'

As well as being a royal sport and pastime, falconry was also used as a method of catching food. The fowler (an individual who used birds of prey to professionally hunt food for the table) could either be employed by a noble person to do his job or could be an independent individual who would make a trade of selling the quarry he'd caught. He would use many devices, including nets, snares, lime, bird-calls and hawks

This juvenile female peregrine falcon is very intently focused on the lure she is pursuing.

to catch his prey. In Aelfic's dialogues, written around AD 1000, the fowler states of his hawks: 'They feed themselves and me in the winter, and in spring I let them fly off to the woods. I catch the young hawks the following autumn and tame them.'

There was a very particular set of rules pertaining to the falconer in the Saxon times. The following are 'The Laws of the Court' as they relate to the falconer:

He is to have his horse in attendance, and his clothing three times in the year, his woolen clothing from the king and his linen clothing from the queen, and his land for free.

His place in the palace is that of fourth man from the king, at mess with him.

His lodgings are the king's barn, lest the smoke from the palace affect his birds.

He is to bring a vessel to the palace to hold his liquor, for he ought only to quench his thirst while in the palace, lest his birds be injured by neglect.

He is to have a hand bredth of wax candle from the steward for feeding his birds and making his bed.

He is not to pay silver to the chief groom, for the king serves him when he flies his hawk, by holding his horse, the time he is to hold his horse is when he alights, and when he mounts to hold the stirrups, and to hold his horse when he performs his necessary duties.

Peregrine tiercel.

He is to have the heart and lungs of the wild animals killed for the kitchens to feed to his hawks.

He is to have an old sheep, or four pence, from the king's villains once a year.

He is to have a third of the dirwy of the falconers [compensation for wrongdoings paid to the king] and the amobyr [maidens fee] of their daughters.

He is to have the skin of a hart in the autumn, and the skin of a hind in the spring to make gloves and jesses.

He is to be honored with three presents on the day his hawk shall kill one of the following three birds – a bittern, a heron, a crane.

He is to have the mantle in which the king shall ride, at the three principal festivals.

His protection is unto the farthest place where he shall fly his hawk at a bird.

He is to have the male hawks, and the nests of the falcons and of the sparrowhawks that are on the king's demesne.

From the time he shall place his hawk in the mew until the time he takes it out, he is not to answer any claim.

His saraas [compensation for insult] is six score of silver.

If the falconers horse is killed, he shall be given another by the king.

If the falconer catches a notable bird, the king must rise and bow to the falconer.

If he does not do so, he must give the clothing he is wearing to the falconer.

Falconry of the Norman Era

The Norman invasion of AD 1066 saw the end of the Anglo-Saxon period in England. The country would never be the same again as a time of great political and social upheaval began.

Records on falconry increased significantly from 1066 onwards, and a wealth of information on how kings and nobles kept their hawks, where they procured them from, and how much falconers were paid, is available from the Norman era.

Duke William, who became King William I of England (otherwise known as William the Conqueror) in 1066 after the Battle of Hastings, was an avid falconer and brought with him from Normandy his Grand Falconer Thurstine de Basset, who, for his service in fighting at the king's side at the Battle of Hastings, was granted his own land in England.

The lanner falcon, a bird from Europe that a Norman falconer would have been familiar with.

William also brought with him a whole team of Flemish falconers under his employment. The Domesday Book lists not only the names but also the land holdings of the individual falconers, and their social standing. It contains some of the first evidence we have of the importation into Britain of the Norway hawk (the Scandinavian goshawk). The list of falconers shows that some of them were originally of Saxon background, so clearly some Saxon men of skill in the field were given employ under Norman subjugation.

In William's time, the title and job of falconer was hereditary, being passed down from father to son for generations and over centuries. The lands that came with the job were also passed down, and as such these individuals were known as serjeanty tenants. At this moment in time, having recently conquered an entire country which was now his for the taking, it was easier for William to pay these professionals with land rather than with sums of money. This was called 'serjeanty'.

We also find listed in the Domesday Book the eyries (nests) of the falcons and hawks. These were protected by law, and landowners and keepers were paid sums to protect and keep a watchful eye over these valuable assets. Records of hawks being used as payment for goods, or in trade deals, also abound. Hawks could also be used to pay the rent, or as a marriage dowry, and vice versa – when hawks were expected to be used as payments, records sometimes show cash payments made in lieu of hawks.

A Norman lady releasing a peregrine falcon in juvenile plumage.

A peregrine falcon named Matilda, in honour of William the Conqueror's wife of the same name.

During the reign of William II there are far fewer references to falconry to be found. However, we do have information about a falconer called Ared, who was notified of the fact that Abbot Godfrey of Malmesbury was given some woodland by William. Ared continued in royal service until the reign of Henry I. He is recorded as owning Chelworth manor in Wiltshire, as well as lands in Oxfordshire.

A single piperoll is all we have to tell us about falconry during the reign of King Henry II. This piperoll gives us more insight into the concept of hawks being paid in lieu. Hawks were owed to the monarch for a variety of reasons, including payment for causing manslaughter, land given, and even to allow a son to take over a father's holdings.

King Stephen's rival, Empress Matilda, was evidently a practicing falconer. Walter Map tells a story about her son, King Henry II, and he says:

> I have heard that his mother's teaching was to this effect, that he should spin out all the affairs of everyone, hold long in his own hands all posts that fell in, take the revenues out of them, and keep the aspirants to them hanging on in hope, and she supported this advice by this unkind parable – An unruly hawk, if meat is often offered to it, and then snatched away or hid, becomes keener and more inclinably obedient and attentive.

A Norman falconer in the woods with a small falcon.

Henry II acceded to the throne in 1154 and triggered the beginning of a new age in falconry. Henry was probably the most ardent of the Norman royal falconers. Peter of Blois spoke of Henry, saying, 'He was an avid lover of the woods, when he ceased from warfare he occupied himself with birds and dogs.' According to Walter Map, 'The King was a great connoisseur of hounds and hawks, and most greedy of that

Manfred, a juvenile peregrine falcon.

vain sport.' Giraldus Cambrensis noted of the king that he 'derived a great deal of pleasure from the flights of birds of prey.'

Henry was such a passionate falconer that he would travel his realm in search of the best sporting flights. There are three famous stories of Henry's exploits in the falconry world.

The hawk and the falcon

While travelling in Wales, hunting with one of his favourite birds, the Norway hawk (goshawk), he spied a stunning peregrine falcon perched atop a rocky crag on the cliffs. The peregrine falcons of Wales are said to be the largest in Britain, and, with this notable quality, Henry decided to launch his Norway hawk into the sky to see an aerial battle between the two! Much to Henry's surprise, the falcon killed the prized royal hawk. It was said that, from that moment onwards, each year at nesting time, King Henry II would send out falconers to trap him some of the falcons from that very area, especially from that cliff, having found none so noble nor so excellent anywhere else in the realm.

The hawk and the heron

Early in in his reign, when still finding his feet as king, and trying to establish himself as a ruler, Henry decided to show off by thrusting his best hawk skyward at the largest heron in the sky – as much for the hunt, and the prestigious social standing he would receive should his bird bring down such a beast, as it was for the sheer enjoyment of it. The hawk was incredibly quick and true to its purpose, striving for the heights, its fleet wings carrying it forth. Certain of imminent capture, the king said, 'That heron will not escape now! Not even if God himself should command it!' Almost as soon as the king had spoken thus, the heron turned and miraculously the prey became the predator. With its beak, the heron 'broke open the hawk's head, causing its brain to be cast out.' The heron, with a look of power and majesty, and completely unharmed, threw down the dying hawk at the king's feet, and continued on its way.

The hawk and the archbishop

Unknown to Henry at the time, when being trained by the Royal Falconer, Ralph de Hauville, the king's prized falcon 'Wiscard' was wounded by a crane it had been pursuing. The falconer, in a panic and knowing his king would be distraught to lose his favourite bird, rushed home and appealed to St Thomas Becket to intercede with God and save the bird.

That night, St Thomas appeared to Ralph in his dreams and told him that there were twelve ulcers on the bird, and that he must open them all and cleanse and drain them to heal the bird. The falconer did as commanded and almost immediately the bird opened his eyes and called out to the falconer for food. When King Henry was told the story, he thanked the martyred St Thomas Becket for his intercession in saving the favourite hunting companion of the king's sporting hours!

Medieval Falconry – Richard I to Richard III (1189–1485)

What could be classed as the crucial major development in European falconry was the advent of the Sixth Crusade, which occurred in 1228/29 when Emperor Frederick II Hohenstaufen, king of Sicily, Jerusalem and Holy Roman Emperor, travelled across the Eastern Mediterranean. Frederick was possibly the most passionate falconer of the medieval era and was also fascinated by Arabic culture.

In this, the early medieval period, the older and harsher techniques of the Saxon and Norman period, in which birds food intake was reduced in order to encourage training, were dropped in favour of the Arabic-style methodologies, in which birds were trained by treating them with respect, by spending a longer period conditioning the bird to become used to its falconer while maintaining its condition with good-quality foodstuffs, and by flying them in as much of a fit, healthy condition as possible.

A medieval woman recalling a kestrel to the fist.

Frederick's Arabic teacher, who passed on to him the eastern falconry skills, was Fakhr ad-Din al-Farsi, who was a Persian advisor to the sultan. He moved to the Sicilian court to work as an advisor and diplomat. Frederick was a keen ornithologist – he was fascinated by the science behind birds, not only birds of prey but all avian species, and he conducted many experiments, such as testing to see if sunlight alone was enough to incubate eggs.

Finally, in the 1240s Frederick wrote his epic manuscript relating to falconry *De Arte Venandi cum Avibus*, or *The Art of Hunting with Birds*. It was filled with hundreds of pages and images relating to the immense knowledge he possessed regarding falconry, and covered all aspects of the captive management and training of birds of prey, especially falcons.

He was the first to introduce the large gyrfalcon from Scandinavia to the world of Mediterranean falconry, and the relationship that he founded between western and eastern falconry was the catalyst for the evolution of falconry techniques across the world.

In Britain, our earliest medieval kings were equally as passionate about falconry and were also travelling out to the east on crusade and finding themselves mind-blown by the Arabic culture and advances in learning in the east.

The saker falcon, favoured bird of the Arabic falconers.

Peregrine tiercel in flight.

The sons of the Norman King Henry II were both passionate falconers. King Richard the Lionheart (Richard I) was an avid falconer who took his hawks and falcons with him to the Holy Land. He often asked envoys from Salah-al-Din to provide him with chickens to feed his hawks, and Richard was famed for going on hunting expeditions with Arabic diplomats. In fact, even when he was taken prisoner by the Duke of Austria, he sent for English falconers to bring him birds from home so he could continue to practice the sport.

His younger brother, King John, enjoys a villainous reputation, but he was an equally passionate falconer as his father, Henry II, and his brother, Richard I. He put laws in place stating that no man may take a wild bird except with his permission. He had a close trade relationship with the King of Norway, who would often send him gifts of his favourite birds, the Norwegian goshawk.

However, John was also surprisingly generous and would give money and alms to people who found lost falconry birds, and also gave out sums to paupers when his birds caught notable prey. He had an establishment of eleven chief falconers. His son, King Henry III, was not a very passionate falconer, preferring to keep a pair of gyrfalcons as pets, which he named Blakeman and Refuse. King John's daughter, Isabella, actually married Emperor Frederick II.

King Richard I.

In the mid-medieval period, King Edward I was the most avid falconer of the time. In just one year, he spent over £1,000 on falconry and constructed the Great Mews at Charing Cross at a cost of £525. He took a very active part in the training of his birds, often communicating with his falconer, Robert de Bavent, by letter, giving firm instructions on how he wanted the birds to be managed.

He would frequently give and receive birds of prey as gifts from other monarchs throughout the world, including the Mongolian Kahn. He treated his professional falconers well – they received a wage, food, somewhere to live, clothing, horses, wax, candles and even wine. His grandson, King Edward III, also loved the sport, so much so that he took fifty falconers with him to France when he entered into the battles of the Hundred Years War.

In the late medieval period, the kings were no less passionate. King Henry IV was a man who thrived on outdoor pursuits, being a brilliant jouster, fighter, huntsman and falconer. He unfortunately suffered ill health from stress and depression at court, so often escaped by going hunting, and he built hunting lodges across the kingdom. The hunting treatise *The Master of Game* was written by Edward of Norwich during Henry IV's reign.

His son, King Henry V, was also a masculine individual who was well-built and who derived great pleasure and enjoyment from warfare and falconry. He enjoyed travelling the countryside in the realm, practicing the pursuits of falconry and hunting

A depiction of a goshawk killing a fowl from a fourteenth-century Italian manuscript.

as he went. He understood that falconry was a good activity to help improve his skill in battle and also practiced throwing javelins and playing tennis to add to his skill.

The Wars of the Roses in the late 1400s saw a new branch of the Plantagenet family sitting on the throne, and the first of the House of York kings was Edward IV, who was another man that could boast immense physical strength and fortitude and great military ability. He was the first king to have been raised as a 'renaissance man' – an individual who was given an education that intertwined all of the art forms, such as dancing, martial arts, horsemanship, leadership, poetry, astronomy and, of course, falconry. His wife, Elizabeth Woodville, who was the first commoner-queen of England, was also a keen falconer.

The last of the medieval kings, Richard III, was a passionate huntsman who loved falconry. Shortly before his death at the Battle of Bosworth in 1485, he had lost both his wife and son to illness. To help him recover from this blow, his good friend John Howard, the Duke of Norfolk, arranged for them to go hunting at Bestwood Park, which was a hunting retreat of around 3,000 acres in Sherwood Forest, a little to the north of Nottingham. Richard found consolation in the art of falconry; his most favoured species of bird to fly were the goshawk and the peregrine.

On 8 March 1485, Richard sent a commission to John Montyguy, who held the title of Seargeant of the Hawks. His request was for John to procure and purchase at cost 'tiercells [male falcons or hawks] and almaner other hawkes as by him shal be thoughte convienient for the kinges disportes.' Following this, on 11 March another commission was given to a John Gaynes to travel abroad with four others to find more hawks for the king, and on the twenty-seventh of the same month Watier Bothnam was given similar orders to find birds from Wales and the Welsh Marches.

This photograph shows the synonymous relationship between falconer and his bird through the almost matching postures they are taking while the bird is being flown.

A saker falcon cruising in to the lure.

However, at the same time Richard's rival, Henry Tudor, who was descended from an illegitimate line of the royal family, had been gathering support and was on his way across the channel from Brittany with plans to invade. By 12 August 1485, he had landed in South Wales and had marched as far as Shrewsbury, gaining more support along the way.

On the 15 August, a few days after Richard arrived at Bestwood, he received word of Henry's arrival, and so on 19 August Richard had to leave Bestwood and make his way across the country towards Leicester. The forces met on the 22 August 1485 and Richard was killed in the following battle after leading the last armoured cavalry charge in British battle history. He never had the chance to train and fly his new birds, and we can only assume that the usurping Henry Tudor at some point took possession of this valuable collection of falcons and hawks.

Ironically, Bestwood Hunting Park was set up by King Richard I in the twelfth century, which brings the story of the English falconer-kings full circle.

The second important treatise from the very end of the medieval period was *The Boke of St Albans*, which was written sometime in the 1480s by Dame Juliana Berners, who was Prioress of Sopwell Abbey but had in her youth lived in the court and experienced court life. Her book covered several aspects of learning that a young man at court should be confident with, including heraldry, and also falconry.

The most famous extract from the book is a listing of birds according to social standing. There is, as a result of this, a common misconception in modern times that this was in fact law; that only people of certain ranks were permitted to fly certain species of bird. This is in fact a myth – an individual in medieval society could fly whichever species of bird their financial situation allowed.

An image of King Henry VII.

It is now thought that the list was more of a satire of medieval society as a whole. For example, the proud and haughty earl is likened to a noble peregrine falcon, whereas the Holy Water Clerk (who was no doubt a nervous individual owing to the stresses of waiting upon the bishops!) were assigned the equally skittish and highly strung sparrowhawk.

The Gyrfalcon and the tiercel [male] of a Gyrfalcon belong to a King.

The Falcon Gentle [a species of Peregrine of most noble features] and the tiercel gentle be for a Prince.

The Falcon of the Rock [probably a Barbary Falcon, which is called Jebal Shaheen in its native territories, which means Rock Falcon] is for a Duke.

The Falcon Peregrine is for an Earl.

The Bastarde [a bird of unknown breeding and lineage and therefore of unknown quality] is for a Baron.

The Saker Falcon and the sacret [male Saker] are for a Knight.

The Lanner Falcon and the lannerette [male Lanner] belong to a Squire.

There is the Merlin Falcon and that is for a Lady.

The Hobby falcon is a falcon for a Young Man.

There is a Goshawk, and that is for a Yeoman.

There is a tiercel [male Goshawk] and that is for a Polebearing man.

There is a Sparrowhawk and he is the hawk for a Priest.

There is a Musket [male Sparrowhawk] and he is for a Holy Water Clerk.

The medieval period opened the doors for the learning and skills to come flooding in from the Middle East and heralded a time of great upheaval as falconers moved from the basic techniques practiced by the early British falconers to the sophisticated and conscientious methods practiced by their Arabic cousins.

A peregrine tiercel, displaying the fine wingspan that gives falcons the nickname 'longwings'.

The Golden Age of Falconry – The Tudor Era

The Tudor period stretched from 22 August 1485, following Henry Tudor's victory at the Battle of Bosworth in which his hired mercenaries defeated and killed the last medieval king of England, Richard III, and it finished with the death of Queen Elizabeth I in 1603.

The Tudor dynasty brought with them the 'Golden Age' of British falconry, moreover because their reign also saw a 118-year-long period of relative peace and stability in Britain after the horrors of the Wars of the Roses. Money was far more plentiful and time and resources could be put into more gentile and noble pursuits like hunting and falconry.

In this time of great peace and prosperity, great unfortified houses began springing up all over the countryside, each with vast swathes of hunting land, and they were designed in such a way as to make a grand statement of wealth, prosperity and power.

As a perfect accompaniment to these impressive properties, their high-class owners would stage entertainments for their guests to demonstrate their social standing, such as jousting tournaments, pageants and falconry expeditions. To be able to show off a stunning collection of valuable hawks and falcons, procured from across the four corners of the globe at great expense, was the perfect way to make a big impression, not only on visiting friends but also to envoys and diplomats sent from foreign allies and enemies.

However, a Tudor hunt was more than just the flying of birds. Hunting hounds were required to hunt and point quarry for the birds to mark and attack, and horses were needed to transport the falconers, all of which required kennel-men and grooms and attendants who all required a wage and accommodation. In this manner, falconry in the Tudor period was simultaneously an enjoyable leisure activity and being a stern and salutary political statement.

The first Tudor king, Henry VII, as previously mentioned, had taken the throne in battle against King Richard III in 1485. His claim to the throne was very weak – he came from an illegitimate branch of the royal family which had been barred from the succession. Shortly after Henry took the throne, a rival claimant

Montacute House, a late Elizabethan show of ostentatiousness.

The parkland at Montacute House as seen today. Acres of land like this would have been set aside for use as hunting parks for nobles and their guests.

A Tudor lady stooping a falcon to the lure.

The colouring of this mature female peregrine would have made her a valuable falcon.

appeared in the form of a young lad called Lambert Simnel. He was said to be the son of a carpenter from Oxfordshire who had been schooled to impersonate the Earl of Warwick as he had a close physical resemblance to him, and the earl was, as the nephew of Richard III, a legitimate claimant to the throne. Simnel was so convincing in his role playing of the Earl of Warwick that he even went as far as rallying troops in Ireland to attempt to take the throne from Henry Tudor. In May 1487, Henry decisively defeated the uprising at the Battle of Stoke.

Henry, however, was very lenient with Lambert Simnel as he saw the boy as merely a pawn of more traitorous individuals. He showed him great mercy by giving him the job of a spit boy in the royal kitchens, rather than imprisoning or executing him. In time Simnel demonstrated not only a loyalty towards the new Tudor regime, but also a natural skill in the training of birds of prey, and eventually he was promoted to Royal Falconer for King Henry VII. He stayed in this employment until he died.

Henry VII created laws which forbade all hunting within the grounds of Westminster Palace, with the exception of his own practices of falconry. He was also greatly concerned with protecting the supplies of native hawks and falcons and so introduced more laws to protect nesting birds, which made the taking of young fledglings a crime.

By the time Henry died in 1509, his eldest son Prince Arthur had already passed away and Arthur's young wife, Catherine of Aragon, had been left a widow for some time. So when Arthur's younger brother, Henry, took the throne as King Henry VIII, he also took Catherine to be his wife and queen.

Catherine was the daughter of two of the greatest monarchs of the renaissance – Isabelle of Castile and Ferdinand of Aragon. Ferdinand was an obsessive falconer himself and died on 23 January 1516 from a chill he had picked up while hawking. Isabella had very little formal education of her own but had hired the very best Italian tutors for all of her children, and as a result Catherine and her sisters became some of the best-educated and learned women in Europe at the time.

King Henry VII, shown with his son King Henry VIII and his third queen, Jane Seymour.

Courtly skills were taught equally alongside Latin and domestic skills, as well as falconry, horsemanship and hunting. By the time Catherine came to England at the age of sixteen to marry Prince Arthur, she was already a very experienced falconer.

Later in life, while heavily pregnant with a child of King Henry VIII, she still continued to practice the art against medical advice, evidenced by the fact that in July 1518 she and King Henry went out hawking in Sir John Perchy's Park for a day.

Henry VIII himself was the most obsessive falconer-king of the age. He had falconry mews situated all over the country so that he could practice the sport when on progress, and at the Great Mews at Charing Cross he had over 300 hawks and falcons situated in areas surrounded by iron fences and guarded by bull mastiff dogs. His yearly expenditure on falconry must have been an epic sum indeed.

Henry was a great exhibitionist. As the younger brother, he had not been destined to be king, instead he had been groomed for a career in the church. However, once he had ascended to the throne, he lost no time in proving himself to be worthy of the title, spending out lavishly from his father's fortune on grand tournaments, banquets and hunting expeditions, which sometimes lasted for several days and were accompanied by entire travelling-kitchen establishments, vast tented accommodation, and swathes of guests and visitors.

A Tudor lady.

King Henry VIII.

A collection of letters exist written by Arthur Plantagenet (Lord Lisle) and his family, known as 'the Lisle Letters'. They give a good insight into Henry's activities – in one such letter, written to Lord Lisle by William Kingston on 26 September 1533, Kingston says of Henry, 'The King hawks every day with the goshawk and with other hawks, that is to say, Lanners, Sparrowhawks, and Merlins, both afore noon, and after if the weather serves.'

Training all of these birds could obviously not be done by the king alone, for it would take vast amounts of time and the king had many other affairs to tend to, and so, although we do have evidence that Henry spent some time involved in the training of his favourite and most-prized birds, we know he also hired many master falconers and under-falconers to train and keep his birds, and manage his mews establishments.

The most famous of these is probably Robert Cheseman, MP, who was born in 1485 and was the son and heir to Edward Cheseman, who had been keeper of the wardrobe to Henry VII. Robert Cheseman held a high position in the Tudor court as an MP and he had presided in the trial of Thomas Cromwell and also in the case involving the infidelities of Henry's fifth wife, Catherine Howard.

One tale is told of a hawking adventure, upon which Henry almost died while out hawking. He had attempted to follow his falcon by pole-vaulting a muddy ditch. However, at the time, Henry was a tall, athletic and muscular man of over 6 feet

The lanner falcon, a bird which King Henry VIII evidently enjoyed flying.

A Henrician lady recalls her falcon to the lure.

in height, and the pole gave way under his weight, leaving him stuck head-first in the muddy sediment of the ditch, suffocating. Rumour has it that it was Robert Cheseman who pulled him out, although alternative sources say it was an old cadger man (a man who carries the 'cadge' – a heavy wooden frame designed to transport several falcons at one time).

Henry believed that hunting was the best means to avoid 'idlenes, the ground of all vyce, and to excersise that thing that shall be honorable and to the bodye healthfull and profitable.' His love of hunting is also evident from the ballad 'Pastimes with Good Company', which he wrote about enjoyable times spent hunting with special and memorable comrades.

His second wife, Anne Boleyn, chose the symbol of a crowned falcon holding a sceptre and perched on a tree stump with red and white roses sprouting forth from the ground. The white falcon crest derived from the heraldic crest of the Earls of Ormonde. Her father, Thomas Boleyn, had been recognised as the heir to the earldom. The heraldic symbol of the falcon represents one who will not rest until their objective is achieved, which is mirrored in Anne's determination to hold off from becoming Henry's mistress in preference of waiting and becoming his queen. It also signifies someone who is eager in pursuit of their goals. The crest was later adopted by Henry and Anne's daughter, Queen Elizabeth I.

'Pastimes with Good Companye' – a hunting ballad written by King Henry VIII.

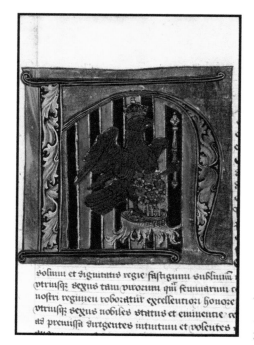

The colour of the falcon demonstrated the mighty gyrfalcon, which was seen as a representation of the pinnacle of nobility and royalty. By choosing such an ostentatious crest, Anne was making an outrageous political statement, which set her as equal to the king. Anne began to use the crest at her coronation, at which point in time she was heavily pregnant, hence the springing Tudor roses bursting forth from the ground in the depiction, watched over carefully by the mighty gyr.

During Anne's coronation, a young child spoke words that had been written by Nicholas Udall to celebrate the event:

> Honour and grace be to our Queen Anne, for whose cause and angel celestial descendeth, the falcon as white as the swan, to crown with a diadem imperial! In her honour, rejoice we all, for it cometh from God and not of man. Honour and grace be to our Queen Anne!

The message in this was that it was God himself who had sent an angel to personally crown Anne, and that this angel was in the form of the noble gyrfalcon.

Udall also penned another ballad about Anne Boleyn, and again she is symbolised as the majestic white falcon:

> Of body small,
> Of power regal,
> She is, and sharp of sight.

The author representing Anne Boleyn at a public demonstration.

Of courage halt,
no manner fault,
Is in this falcon white

The falcon, as Anne's symbol, shows her to be someone who is not only steadfast in achieving their goal, but also someone who demands respect and is equal to the king himself. She was in fact not typical of ladies of her day, she was a very outgoing and would spend entire days in the field hunting and hawking alongside the king. Henry was very proud of the fact that he could easily tire five horses out during the course of a day's hunting exploits, but it was said that Anne was not only a match for the king but could in fact outdo him. Like her predecessor, Catherine of Aragon, Anne Boleyn had also experienced a foreign education, in France. During her time living at the court there she had learnt how to ride, hunt and hawk. It was these skills, alongside her intelligence and charm, with which she caught the eye of the king.

Jane Seymour was Henry's third wife and she took his attention while he was staying at her family home, Wolf Hall, for a hunting expedition in the nearby Savernake Forest in 1535, while Henry was still married to Anne Boleyn.

Jane had not been raised for life at court, and had not received anywhere near the quality of education enjoyed by either Catherine or Anne. However, she had been raised as a country gentlewoman and she was an expert horsewoman. Hunting was one of her favourite pursuits as a young girl, and also after she became queen.

A young peregrine enjoying a meal of quail on the falconers fist.

Henry's fourth wife, Anne of Cleves, was also a very keen hunts-woman. Although her relationship with Henry was a disastrously short-lived affair, her acquiescence to the divorce Henry soon requested allowed her to maintain a close and friendly relationship with the king, who termed her to be his 'sister'. She was given the home once belonging to the Boleyn family prior to their fall from grace, Hever Castle, and she used it to live out her days in a quiet fashion, enjoying the pursuit of falconry within the grounds at her leisure.

Henry's daughter, Elizabeth, was a master huntswoman, which is hardly surprising given the passion for hunting shared by both her father, King Henry VIII, and her mother, Anne Boleyn.

When she ascended to the throne in 1558 there were already laws in place that punished offenders who committed hunting offences. These included hunting in disguise or at night in the royal hunting parks and forests, and also the thefts of eggs and fledglings of falcons or hawks.

Elizabeth reduced the punishments for these offences to three months in prison, payment of treble the value of any damage caused, and a seven-year surety on good behaviour. She also did away with the social ideals relating to falconry, which made owning a prestigious species of bird more accessible to less noble individuals.

Her favourite confidant, friend and Master of Horse, Lord Robert Dudley, was an obsessive huntsman and falconer, and he and Elizabeth often disappeared for

A portrait of the Tudor dynasty, showing Queen Elizabeth I alongside her father, King Henry VIII, her sister Queen Mary I, and young brother, King Edward VI.

Lord Robert Dudley, first Earl of Leicester, Knight of the Garter and Elizabeth I's confidante and Master of Horse, who was known for his love of the peregrine falcon and the Barbary falcon.

whole days together to enjoy the sport of hunting with hawks. Dudley was the first person in Britain to train setting dogs for hunting, pointing and retrieving, which is the style which is commonly used today. His favourite hunting bird was the peregrine falcon and his most-loved style of hunting was known as 'hawking at the brook' – using highly trained birds to catch heron, crane and swan, which were said to be the most noble quarry of all. It offered extremely sporting flights, with one or other bird attempting to gain height until either the falcon could get higher, to then stoop down on her prey, or the noble heron could escape. A peregrine falcon that excelled at this sport was an extremely sought after and highly prized bird.

However, the biggest problem with the peregrine falcon, as Dudley was well aware, is their tendency to shirk, meaning to leave their initial quarry for an easier target. Peregrines, like most other predatory animals, are instinctively programmed to go for the weak, sick, or injured quarry as they are an easier kill. In the wild, this allows for a greater chance of species survival as a broken feather or bone on the falcon, sustained in a tussle, could easily mean the difference between life and death.

As Master of Horse to Queen Elizabeth, Dudley was commissioned with sourcing and importing horses of the highest quality for her stables. He prized the

An Elizabethan gentleman returning from a successful flight.

A juvenile Barbary falcon, displaying exquisite markings on his plumage.

Barbary horses for their speed and agility, and in his later life he set up the Barbary Company to import commodities back from the Barbary Coast of North Africa.

It was during this work, and through the travels and studies of his friend George Tuberville, who was a professional falconer, that he came across the Barbary falcon (*Falco Pelegrinoides*). This beautiful little falcon is considerably smaller in stature than the peregrine, but in comparison is highly aggressive on the wing and does not have the same tendency to shirk away from its prey. Dudley and Tuberville are some of the earliest falconers in Britain to have officially introduced and flown this charming little bird.

Dudley saw worth in them for two reasons – firstly their innate aggression on the hunt, which would reflect on the falconer and demonstrate to others that the falconer was a force to be reckoned with, but also their charming personalities and friendliness towards their falconer and, more importantly, the fact that politically they demonstrated the world-power that Queen Elizabeth enjoyed through her trade relationships abroad. Considering that she had a tenuous grip on the throne, owing to the breakdown in the relationship between her parents that saw her cast out as illegitimate, it was worth her while demonstrating her power in any way that she could. Elizabeth often used hunting and hawking as a way of proving that she was her father's true daughter and worthy to sit upon the throne. In front of visiting dignitaries and ambassadors, she would hunt as a man, sitting astride her horse. She would also personally hunt for great red deer stags, which she would

Above and left: An Elizabethan gentleman with a young Barbary falcon, the favourite bird of Robert Dudley.

slit the throats of, and practiced the ancient ritual of 'blooding' herself and her fellow huntsmen with the blood of the kill, daubing her face with it. She was also a capable archer, with the ability to string and loose a bow of a poundage that many modern men would struggle with.

Dudley was a key figure of this era and is given barely any credit not only for his undivided and constant loyalty to Elizabeth and to England, but also for his love of hunting. After the Armada, at which he commanded the standing army at Tilbury, he retired to Buxton in Oxfordshire to recover from a stomach ailment. He died there in 1588 at fifty-five years of age.

Queen Elizabeth is said to have never truly recovered from the blow of his loss, and kept the last letter that he wrote to her a few days before he died, which she marked out in her own handwriting as 'His Last Letter', keeping it wrapped around a miniature portrait of him, both of which remained locked safely in her trinket box with all of her most prized possessions until she died in 1603.

It impossible to discuss Tudor falconry without mentioning the two incredibly famous treatises that were written during that age.

The first of these is *The Treatise on the Shortwinged Hawk*, which was written by Edmund Bert in the late 1500s and finally published in 1619. This small book contains all the necessary information required, including step-by-step instructions for completing the intensive manning required for a goshawk. He also describes the 'Waking Process', in which the bird is kept with the austringer for several days. During this period neither sleep, meaning they can bond with each other and the normally skittish and untame hawk, through exhaustion and vulnerability, can finally realise that the austringer has not harmed her and has in fact offered it good doses of fine-quality food, thus beginning to earn the trust of the bird. Mention is made of the necessity to keep the bird indoors with the austringer so that the bird can, over time, become better accustomed to the sights and sounds of the household, people coming and going, and other working animals such as dogs.

An addendum work to Edmund Bert's treatise is a short addition called *The Perfect Boke for keepyng Sparrowhawks*, which was written by an unknown author in 1575 and was penned with the training of the smaller accipiter in mind. It has a wealth of information about medicine and cures for the birds, some of which are very strange indeed. Some of the treatments have ingredients which may have had positive, curative, effects, but others would almost certainly have served to make the hawk worse. One such example as a possibly effective cure is that designed for a case of gout in the bird. They suggested 'a little galbanum' alongside 'turpentine, and a good quantity of red or yellow wax', which was to be administered to the leg to draw out swelling. While at first this may sound strange, galbanum is an aromatic herb that has potential anti-bacterial properties, and turpentine is made from a substance found in pine needles, which are used by wild birds to blanket their nesting sites due to their anti-fungal properties. However, a rather more

AN APPROVED TREATISE OF
Hawkes and Hawking.

Divided into three Bookes.

The firſt teacheth, How to make a ſhort-winged Hawke good, with good conditions.
The ſecond, How to reclaime a Hawke from any ill condition.
The third, teacheth Cures for all knowne griefes and diſeaſes.

By EDMVND BERT, *Gentleman.*

LONDON,
Printed by *T. S.* for *Richard Moore*, and are to be ſold at his ſhop in S. *Dunſtans* Church-yard.
1619.

The frontispiece to Edmund Bert's treatise on the shortwinged hawk, written in the late 1500s during the reign of Queen Elizabeth I and published in 1619.

negative remedy suggested mixing arsenic with capon grease and vinegar, and feeding it to the bird!

The second famous treatise of the Elizabethan court was written in the late 1500s by George Tuberville, who was a falconer and friend to Robert Dudley. This treatise is a collection of the experiences of many European falconers whom Tuberville met on his travels abroad. It was known as falconry or hawking and it covered the various species of bird available to Tudor falconers, their pros and cons, and the training of a falcon.

Perhaps the most famous of Queen Elizabeth I's falconers was Sir Ralph Sadler. Ralph had grown up as a ward of Thomas Cromwell, who had been a lawyer to Henry VIII. Ralph showed an especial skill in falconry and was promoted to the job as a professional falconer at court. Ralph's son inherited the skills from his father, and he appears in the next chapter ...

An adult female peregrine falcon.

Lanner falcon.

This male barabary falcon is mid-moult, displaying the colourful transition between juvenile and adult plumage.

The English Civil War – Falconry, Cavaliers and Roundheads

The author, Andrew, stooping a juvenile female peregrine falcon to the lure in royalist Civil War attire.

Falconry suffered a bit of a decline shortly after the Tudor era, and by the time of the English Civil War it was not as popularly practiced as it had once been. This was, firstly, because huntsmen were starting to use guns, rather than hawks and falcons, as guns had evolved to be more accurate and were certainly a far cheaper and easier way of catching quarry and showing ones wealth, and secondly because the land was beginning to be enclosed, which made the pursuit of a lost or hunting bird increasingly more difficult.

However, despite this there were those who continued to practice the sport, not least King Charles I, and the Lord Protector, Oliver Cromwell.

Lewis Latham was the Sergeant Falconer to King Charles I. He was born in 1584 during the reign of Queen Elizabeth I and he died on 15 May 1655. At the start of his career he was falconer to a man named Richard Bernick, before later becoming an under-falconer to Charles when he was still a prince.

When Charles succeeded to the throne in 1625, Latham was given the position of Sergeant Falconer to the king. Evidence of his service can be found within the Calendars of State Papers:

1625: July 15h – Warrant to pay Andrew Pitcairn, Master of the Hawkes to the use of Lewis Latham, Eustace Norton, and the rest of the under-falconers the stipend formally allowed them when the king was Prince of Wales.

Lewis was the half-brother of Simon Latham, who was also a falconer and who penned the three editions of *Latham's Falconry*, which was published in two books in 1618 and re-edited in 1633 and 1652.

Lewis Latham worked under Charles I's Master Falconer, Sir Patrick Home. Home employed a total of thirty-three under-falconers.

A portrait showing Charing Cross as it appeared during the reign of King Charles I. The mews, housing the hawks and falcons, were accessed through the intricate building seen on the right hand side in the distance.

A miniature showing a young Charles, dating from a time when he was still Prince of Wales.

Carolus Primus D.G. Anglia Scotia Francia et Hibernia Rex &c.

An image of King Charles I.

A later extract from the Calendars of State Papers reads, '1627, Aug 18th – Warrant from secretary Conway to Anthony General Heath, to prepare grants of the place of Sergeant of the Hawks to Lewis Latham.'

Lewis's half-brother, Simon, had been born in 1576 and died on 19 May 1649. Simon had learnt falconry from another falconer, Henry Sadler of Everley Wiltshire, who happened to be the son of Ralph Sadler, previously mentioned in the chapter covering Tudor falconry.

The 1600s saw the end of the zenith of falconry in Britain. The Civil War involved almost all of the nobility of the realm and, as such, people couldn't afford to practice the opulent sports that had been enjoyed in the more peaceful times of the Tudor era. While falconry had been a way of demonstrating one's wealth, by the end of the 1600s it was just as easy to demonstrate to society the height of one's social standing with a fine-quality rifle, rather than keeping the great retinues of falconers that were required for hawking exploits.

While Oliver Cromwell had banned many forms of entertainment, such as fine clothing, theatre and even Christmas, he loved hunting, believing it to be a grand form of physical exercise.

After the 1600s, when fields began to be enclosed, it became even more difficult to practice the sport. By the start of the 1700s the skills practiced by historical falconers had all but died a death in Britain.

A portrait from 1660s showing a selection of dead game animals alongside a hunting bag and falconry hoods.

A royalist falconer must have cut a dashing figure. This royalist falconer is carrying a saker falcon.

Oliverus Cromwell

Oliver Cromwell, Lord Protector.

A royalist lady in upper-class attire admiring her falcon.

A Civil War gentleman recalling a young peregrine to the fist after a successful first flight.

Lanner falcon turning.

Full Circle – The Victorians and the Advent of 'Modern' Falconry

Throughout the Georgian period in the 1700s there were still a few die-hard traditionalists in the nobility who practiced the sport, but it was no longer held in any form of prestige. By the time of the Victorian period, the skills used in falconry had changed so much that the famous falconers of the past would have barely recognised it.

Treatises regarding falconry from the mid- to late Victorian period describe techniques that begin to resemble the food reduction or weight management techniques that are used today. It is almost as if falconry skills had gone 'full circle', back to a time before we had garnered the learning and advanced techniques from the Middle East.

Painting of a niche showing a collection of falconry equipment dating to the late 1600s showing various items used by a falconer.

The Victorian era saw the birth of the Royal Loo Hawking Club, the founder of which was Prince Alexander of the Netherlands. He was an obsessive hunter and horseman and he had received permission from his grandfather, the king, to reinstate falconry as a noble art at Het Loo. He became the chairman of the Hawking Club, which held regular meets at Het Loo made up of international noblemen.

Falconry today, in the twenty-first century, has become a very scientific affair. The bird of prey is viewed as a hunting tool, incapable of emotional feeling or bonding, and its captive management involves a rather distanced and scientific approach involving the daily weighing, weight charting, and food monitoring approach, to determine whether the bird is in a condition to fly. Birds are housed away from the falconers and as such, contact between the falconer and their bird are at a minimum, even during the training period. Modern falconers are encouraged to reduce the amount of food given as a mode of starting the training of the hawk and are told that a bird will not fly for them unless it is hungry.

By contrast, a historical falconer would keep their bird alongside them throughout the day and night during training, and the bird would be made to feel comfortable with nourishing foods and would gradually learn to trust the falconer. This would later allow the falconer to train the bird at a much higher weight and

A juvenile peregrine tiercel in flight.

condition and yet still find them calm, malleable and responsive. The bird was viewed as a hunting partner to be loved and respected, rather than a tool, and the historical falconer believed the bird was equally as capable of love in return.

These techniques, of course, are far more complex than the simple explanation given above, and deserving of a whole book in their own right.

However, it is clear to see that throughout the medieval and renaissance period, falconry in Britain went through a golden age, a beautiful realisation of a more gentle and natural way of training the birds that was learnt from the Eastern realms, where thousands of years of practice and learning had built up to an inherent understanding of how best to perform captive raptor management. While these methods of practice were forgotten in Britain, they still continue to be used elsewhere in the world, where skills have been passed down from generation to generation, from father to son.

The authors, relaxed after a successful day's flying.

Left: Peregrine.

Below: Mature female peregrine.

© Gareth Howell 2015

Common buzzard.

Glossary

Accipiter: The scientific name for a hawk.

Archaeology: The study of human history via the excavation of historical sites and the analysis of artefacts and remains.

Austringer: The historical term for an individual who trains and flies hawks (*accipiters*).

Baiting/To Bate: The action of a tethered bird, jumping from its perch or off the fist, in an attempt to get away.

Beaker People: A western European culture, dating from 2800 to 1800 BC, which started in the Neolithic era and stretched into the early Bronze Age.

Bronze Age: A period in history, which in Britain spanned from 2500 to 800 BC and was characterised by the findings of weapons and tools made from bronze.

Cist: A stone-built ossuary, often associated with barrows or other monuments, designed to hold the remains of a dead individual.

Captive Management: The management of the training, health and wellbeing of birds of prey by man, when kept permanently housed by man.

English Civil War: A series of armed conflicts that characterised the mid-1600s (1642–1651), stemming from machinations between Parliament and the Monarchy.

Falcon: A long-winged bird of prey, characterised by their high aerial stoops and manoeuvres.

Falconer: An individual who trains and hunts with falcons.

Falconry: The art of keeping, training and managing falcons for the sport of hunting. This term is often used to describe the keeping of hawks also, although correctly it should only be used to describe the flying of falcons.

Fieldsport: A collection of outdoor pursuits, usually involving hunting, such as falconry, shooting, or fishing.

Flush: To push sheltering quarry out of their hiding places and into the open, in order to hunt them, usually achieved by using beaters (humans who hit at cover with sticks) or dogs.

Hawk: A short-winged bird of prey, characterised by their short-burst flights, typically in dense cover.

Iron Age: A period of history, which in Britain stretched from 800 BC to AD 43, characterised by the use of iron tools.

Imprint/Imprinted: A term used by modern falconers to describe the action of taking a very young bird of prey away from the nest and instead of allowing it to be raised by its natural parents, it is raised by humans. This makes the bird believe the humans are its parents and source of food, by which they become dependent on the humans. It was a practice greatly frowned upon by historical falconers, and an imprinted bird was considered, by and large, to be useless.

Jesses: The straps, often made of leather, which allow the falconer to maintain a hold of the bird. The straps are attached to the bird's leg.

Leash: The method of tethering a bird of prey.

Mangalah: A wrist cuff, used by Middle Eastern falconers, instead of a glove.

Medieval Period: A period in Britain that stretched roughly from King Richard I (AD 1189) until the death of King Richard III (AD 1483).

Norman Period: A period in Britain that stretched from the Norman Conquest in 1066 until roughly the death of King Henry II in AD 1189.

Pounces: The claws of a hawk.

Point: The action of a trained dog to signal the presence and whereabouts of quarry.

Quarry: Prey animals.

Raptor: A bird of prey, a bird that feeds on raw meat.

Roman Era: The period of British history when Romans populated the British Isles, from AD 43 until 410.

Scent: The action of a trained dog to use its nose to pick up the trail of quarry using the residual smell of the animal left on the ground.

Shirk: The action of a bird of prey, to decide midway through pursuit of quarry to no longer attempt to bring down the original quarry and to look for easier pickings.

Talons: The claws of a falcon.

Tudor Era: A period of British history, stretching from AD 1485 to 1603.

Treatise: A written work dealing in particular with a specialist subject.

Viking/Saxon Era: The Saxon era in Britain stretched from around AD 500 until the conquest of the Normans in 1066. The Saxon era was interspersed with raids and attacks on Britain from Viking invaders from Scandinavia.

Bibliography

Books

Almond, Richard, *Medieval Hunting* (Stroud: The History Press, 2011).

Ashdown-Hill, John, *The Last Days of Richard III* (Stroud: The History Press, 2010).

Bert, Edmund, *An Approved Treatise Of Hawks And Hawking* (London: T. S. Primters, 1619).

Bukach, David, John Hunter and Ann Woodward, *An Examination of Prehistoric Stone Bracers of Britain* (Oxford: Oxbow, 2011).

Byrne, Muriel, St. Clare, *The Lyle Letters* (Middlesex: Penguin Ltd, 1985).

Cassaday, Richard F., *The Emperor and the Saint* (Illinois: Illinois University Press).

Cummins, John, *The Hound and the Hawk* (London: Palgrave Macmillan, 1988).

Doran, Susan, *The Tudor Chronicles* (London: Quercus, 2008).

Falcus, Christopher, *The Private Lives of the Tudor Monarchs* (London: Folio Society, 1974).

Graham-Campbell, James, *The Vikings* (London: William Morrow, 1980).

Gristwood, Sarah, *Elizabeth and Leycester* (Ealing: Bantom Press, 2007).

Loades, David, *Chronicle of the Tudor Kings* (Worthing: Bramley, 1996).

Magnusson, Magnus, *Vikings* (Book Club Associates, 1980).

Nicolson, Adam, *Arcadia* (London: Harper Perrenial, 2008).

Norton, Elizabeth, *Jane Seymour Henry VIII True Love* (Stroud: Amberley Publishing, 2009).

Norwich, Edward, *Master of Game* (University of Pennsylvania: Penn Press, 2005).

Oggins, Robin, *Kings and Their Hawks* (Yale: Yale University Press, 2004).

Savage, Anne, *The Anglo Saxon Chronicles* (Connecticut: Greenwich Editions, 2002).

Seward, Desmond, *The Last White Rose* (London: Constable and Robinson, 2010).

Starkey, David, Henry, *Virtuous Prince* (London: Harper Press, 2008).

Tremlet, Giles, *Catherine of Aragon* (London: Faber Ltd, 2010).

Wilson, Derek, *Sweet Robin* (London: Alison and Buzby Ltd, 1997).

Archaeological Articles

Cherryson, A. K., 'The Identification Of Archaeological Evidence of Hawking in Medieval England', *Acta Zoological Cracoviensia*, Vol. 45 (Krakow: 29 November 2002) pp. 307–314.

Lukasyk, Ewa, 'Mediterranean Falconry as a Cross Cultural Bridge, Christian-Muslim Hunting Encounters', *Institute for Interdisciplinary Studies*, (Warsaw: 2011).

Prummel, Wielske, 'Evidence of Hawking From Bird and Mammal Bones', *International Journal of Osteoarcheology*, Vol. 7 (Oxford: July/August 1997). pp. 333–338.

Wallis, R. J., 'Re-examining Stone Wrist Guards as Evidence for Falconry in Later Prehistoric Britain', *Antiquity: A Periodical Review of Archaeology* (Cambridge: 2014).

Woodwood, A. J. Hunter, R. Ixer, F. Roe, P. Potts, P. C. Webb, J. S. Watson, M. C. Jones, 'Beaker Age Bracers in England: Sources, Function and Use', *Antiquity: A Periodical Review of Archaeology* (Cambridge: 2006).